Color!

Just Beautiful Coloring Designs

Deb Gilbert

Title: Color! Just Beautiful Coloring Designs
Author: Deb Gilbert
Published by: Heller Brothers Publishing

Copyright © 2016 by Deb Gilbert
Photo Credits: Krivoruchko @depositphotos.com
First Edition, 2016
Published in USA

 All rights reserved. No part of this book may be reproduced or transmitted in any form or by any means, including but not limited to information storage and retrieval systems, electronic, mechanical, photocopy, recording, etc. without written permission from the copyright holder.

ISBN: 978-1-944678-06-7

This Coloring Book Belongs To:

_____

Date Completed: _____
Media Used:_____
_____
_____
Notes: _____
_____
_____
_____
_____

Date Completed: _____
Media Used:_____
_____
Notes: _____
_____
_____
_____

Date Completed: _____
Media Used:_____
_____
_____
Notes: _____
_____
_____
_____
_____

Date Completed: _____
Media Used:_____
_____

Notes: _____
_____
_____
_____
_____

Date Completed: _____
Media Used:_____
_____
_____
Notes: _____
_____
_____
_____
_____

Date Completed: _____
Media Used:_____
_____
Notes: _____
_____
_____
_____
_____

Date Completed: _____
Media Used: _____
_____
_____
Notes: _____
_____
_____
_____
_____

Date Completed: _____
Media Used:_____
_____

Notes: _____
_____
_____
_____

Date Completed: _____
Media Used:_____
_____
_____
Notes: _____
_____
_____
_____
_____

Date Completed: _____
Media Used:_____
_____
_____
Notes: _____
_____
_____
_____
_____

Date Completed: _____
Media Used: _____
_____
_____
Notes: _____
_____
_____
_____
_____

Date Completed: _____
Media Used:_____
_____
_____
Notes: _____
_____
_____
_____
_____

Date Completed: _____
Media Used:_____
_____
_____
Notes: _____
_____
_____
_____
_____

Date Completed: _____
Media Used:_____
_____
_____
Notes: _____
_____
_____
_____
_____

Date Completed: _____
Media Used:_____
_____
_____
Notes: _____
_____
_____
_____
_____

Date Completed: _____
Media Used: _____
_____
_____
Notes: _____
_____
_____
_____
_____

Date Completed: _____
Media Used:_____
_____
_____
Notes: _____
_____
_____
_____
_____

Date Completed: _____
Media Used:_____
_____
_____
Notes: _____
_____
_____
_____
_____

Date Completed: _____
Media Used: _____
_____
_____
Notes: _____
_____
_____
_____
_____

Date Completed: _____
Media Used:_____
_____
_____
Notes: _____
_____
_____
_____
_____

Date Completed: _____
Media Used:_____
_____
_____
Notes: _____
_____
_____
_____
_____

Date Completed: _____
Media Used:_____
_____
_____
Notes: _____
_____
_____
_____
_____

Date Completed: _____
Media Used: _____
_____
Notes: _____
_____
_____
_____
_____

Date Completed: _____
Media Used:_____
_____
_____
Notes: _____
_____
_____
_____
_____

Date Completed: _____
Media Used: _____
_____
_____
Notes: _____
_____
_____
_____
_____

Date Completed: _____
Media Used:_____
_____
_____
Notes: _____
_____
_____
_____
_____

Date Completed: _____
Media Used:_____
_____
_____
Notes: _____
_____
_____
_____
_____

Date Completed: _____
Media Used:_____
_____
_____
Notes: _____
_____
_____
_____
_____

Date Completed: _____
Media Used:_____
_____
_____
Notes: _____
_____
_____
_____
_____

Date Completed: _____
Media Used:_____
_____
_____
Notes: _____
_____
_____
_____
_____

Date Completed: _____
Media Used:_____
_____
_____
Notes: _____
_____
_____
_____
_____

Date Completed: _____
Media Used:_____
_____
_____
Notes: _____
_____
_____
_____
_____

Date Completed: _____
Media Used:_____
_____
_____
Notes: _____
_____
_____
_____
_____

Date Completed: _____
Media Used: _____
_____
_____
Notes: _____
_____
_____
_____
_____

Date Completed: _____
Media Used:_____
_____
_____
Notes: _____
_____
_____
_____

About the Author

Dr. Deb Gilbert has been working from home since 2007 and is an online professor of education, research, and leadership. She has been involved in public schools and higher education for over 25 years and has a passion for promoting literacy. She is the author of several books, journals, and adult coloring books.

For more information on Deb Gilbert, please join her at
www.hellerbrotherspublishing.com
and on Facebook at:
https://www.facebook.com/coloringbookstoheal/

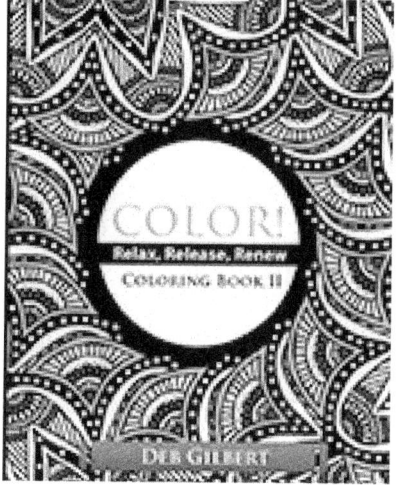

www.ingramcontent.com/pod-product-compliance
Lightning Source LLC
Chambersburg PA
CBHW080942040426
42444CB00015B/3413